Headwork 5

Chris Culshaw and David Craig

Oxford University Press

Acknowledgements

The publishers would like to thank the following for permission
to reproduce photographs:
John Cleare Mountain Camera: p.14 (bottom right);
Format Partners: p.14 (middle);
Spectrum Colour Library: p.14 (top left, right and bottom left);
John Walmsley: p.44, 46.

The illustrations are by Katherine Baxter, Phillip Burrows,
Martin Chatterton, Elitta Fell, Debbie Hinks, Alan Marks, Mike
Nicholson, Jason Pizzey, Viv Quillin, Ursula Sieger.

The cover illustration is by Jason Pizzey.

Oxford University Press, Walton Street, Oxford OX2 6DP

Oxford   New York   Toronto
Delhi   Bombay   Calcutta   Madras   Karachi
Petaling Jaya   Singapore   Hong Kong   Tokyo
Nairobi   Dar es Salaam   Cape Town
Melbourne   Auckland

and associated companies in
Berlin   Ibadan

Oxford is a trade mark of Oxford University Press

© Chris Culshaw and David Craig 1990

First published 1990
Reprinted 1991

ISBN 019 833387 0

Typeset by Tradespools Ltd, Frome, Somerset
Printed in Great Britain by Thomson Litho Ltd, East Kilbride, Scotland

Contents

Use your Head

Thinking about Thinking

A My brain is like a huge hotel with millions of rooms. Each room is full of things I've learned.

B I think my brain is like a computer, but slower. I work things out carefully, step by step.

C I always get in a muddle when I've got a hard problem to think about. My brain is like a pan of spaghetti.

My brain is like an anthill, with millions of tiny passageways. There is always something going on in my head. The ants never seem to rest. D

E My brain is like a naughty puppy! It never does what I want it to do. If I've got Maths homework to do it wants to read a comic or watch television.

My brain is like a massive forest. It's full of amazing ideas. But some of these ideas are like shy animals, they hide away in the middle of the forest. I don't think we can really understand how our brains work. F

2

What to do

Read what the six people said about their brains.
Answer these questions.

1 Which people said something positive (good) about their brain?

2 Which people said something negative (bad)?

3 Which person do you think might be good at creative things like writing stories and songs? Give a reason for this.

4 Which person do you think would be best at working out practical problems? Give a reason.

5 If these six people were in your class or group which one do you think you would choose to work with? Why?

6 Write a few words about how you picture your own brain.

What to do next

Working in pairs or in small groups
Copy and complete the table below. Compare your table with those done by other groups.

		← Copy this part only →		
		Yes	No	Not sure
1	Brains are like car engines. You have to look after them or else they break down.	1			
2	There is no limit to what the human brain can do.	2			
3	There is nothing in your brain when you are born.	3			
4	Girls' brains work faster than boys' brains.	4			
5	A brain is just a computer.	5			
6	Most people only ever use a tiny part of their brain.	6			

3

Seventy Thousand Hours

Billy is 15 years old which means he has been alive and kicking for 5500 days. The average person is awake for 12 hours each day, so this means Billy has been walking about on Planet Earth for nearly 70 000 hours.

Billy thinks he knows 'nothing', but he is wrong. He has seen a lot, heard a lot and learned a lot.

Here is a list of *some* of the things Billy did one Saturday.

Got up, had a shower, cleaned his teeth.
Made his bed.
Cooked bacon and egg for his mum.
Watched television and read the paper.
Went by bus to his grandma's house.
Went to the supermarket for his grandma.
Went into town with his friends.
Went home by bus.
Made lunch for himself and his little sister.
Loaded some washing into the washing machine.
Telephoned his girl-friend.
Mended a puncture on his bike.
Watched television.
Helped his dad make the evening meal.
Went round to his friend's to watch a video.

What to do

1   Make a list of all the machines Billy had to know how to use that Saturday.

2   List all the different kinds of reading Billy had to do.

3   Make a list of all the information Billy needed to do the things he did. Write your list like this:

1 Information about cooking bacon and egg.
2 Information about bus times and bus fares.

What to do next

List the skills and information Billy needs to do these things:

1   Make cheese on toast.

2   Do his paper round.

3   Help his little sister with her Maths homework.

What to do

Working in pairs or in small groups
Make a list of all the skills and information you have used today. Give each one a rating using this scale:

  * = useful
 ** = very useful
*** = vital

Compare your ratings and lists with other groups.

Taking a Trip Round your Brain

In some ways your brain is like a huge city. All the ideas and information in your head are linked together – just like the network of streets and roads in a city.

Some parts of your brain are busy, like the main shopping streets in a town. Other parts of your brain are quiet and mysterious, like dark, narrow lanes.

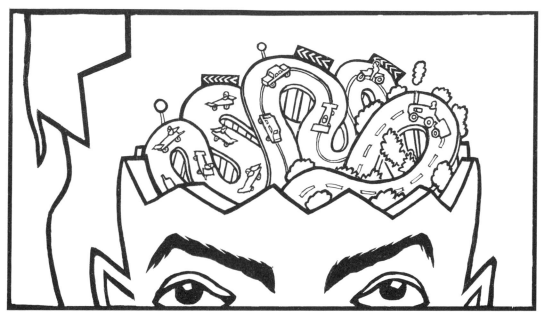

One way to take a trip around the 'streets' in your brain is to play a simple word association game.

Three people were asked to write down what words came into their head when they heard the trigger word 'fishing'.

boat
river
stone
fossil
dinosaur
ice
cream
beach
waves
swim

canal
bridge
road
bus
driver
engine
oil
sea
waves
seaweed

rod
line
washing
soap
television
video
tape
plastic
ball
beach

Each list is like a journey through the streets and lanes of the three brains. Each list gives us some clues about how those streets are linked together.

6

Look at the three lists in the thought bubbles and answer these questions.

1   Why do you think the three lists are different?

2   Can you find any links between the three lists?
    Write your answer like this:

1 River, waves and washing are all to do with water.

3   Is there any way we could predict what will be the last word on someone's list? Give a reason for your answer.

4   If you asked some very young people and some very old people to play this game do you think there would be important differences between their lists? Give a reason for your answer.

5   If you asked 10 000 people to play this game do you think any two people would write *identical* lists? Give a reason for your answer.

┌─ **What to do next** ───

Working in pairs
Each write down the ten words that come into your head when you start with the trigger word 'supermarket'. Compare your lists. Can you find any links between the two lists? Can you explain these links?

Now repeat this exercise using your own trigger words.

Does Know-it-all Know it all?

Know-it-all doesn't know everything of course. He can tell you the answers to questions like: Who won the FA Cup in 1926?

He can name all the queens and kings of England, tell you the longest river in the world or how many eggs an emu lays.

Know-It-All, the well known know-all, sits down for a tasty snack.

But there are many questions he cannot answer. There are lots of important questions that cannot be answered by looking in books. There are many questions that people have chewed over for years and never found out the answers. Sometimes asking the right question is just as important as knowing the right answer. Good questions are like long sharp needles, they go right to the heart of a problem. Good questions make you think.

A teacher set her class the following problem:

> I want you to make up some questions for 'The Hardest Quiz in the World'.

Here are the questions her class made up:

1   What is the most common thing in the world?

2   What is the most valuable thing in the world?

3   Why do people have freckles?

4   Why do people cry?

5   Why do people dream?

6   What is a friend?

7   Why do people believe in gods?

8   Where will evolution end?

9 What is sleep?

10 Why do people get drunk?

11 What do young people worry about most?

12 What, or who, could be called 'Ruler of the Earth'?

13 What, if anything, is free?

14 What makes a good person?

15 What is progress?

What to do

Working in pairs or in small groups
Copy the table below. Classify the quiz questions. Compare your classifications with those of other groups.

Question no.	Possible to answer	Impossible to answer
1		
2		
15		

What to do next

Working in pairs or in small groups
1 Pick one of the questions you classified as 'possible to answer'. Write down what you would need to do to answer this question. Decide who you would need to ask about the problem, where you might look for information, etc.

2 Write some more questions for 'The Hardest Quiz in the World'.

Mr Justin Case

Mr Justin Case is a man who doesn't like to take risks.

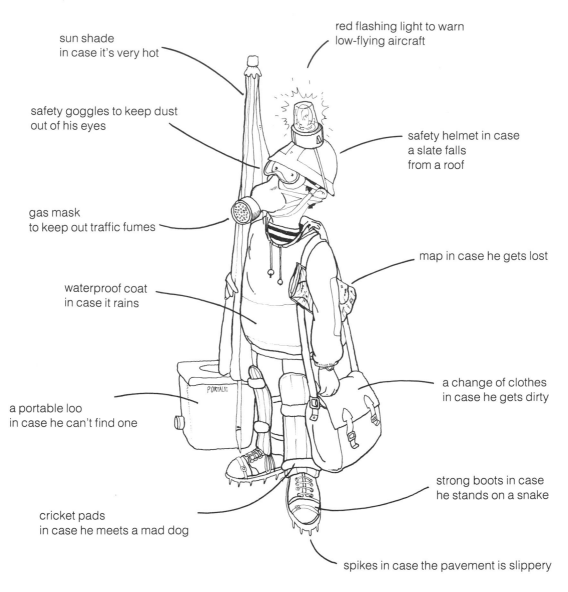

sun shade
in case it's very hot

red flashing light to warn
low-flying aircraft

safety goggles to keep dust
out of his eyes

safety helmet in case
a slate falls
from a roof

gas mask
to keep out traffic fumes

map in case he gets lost

waterproof coat
in case it rains

a portable loo
in case he can't find one

PORTALOO

a change of clothes
in case he gets dirty

cricket pads
in case he meets a mad dog

strong boots in case
he stands on a snake

spikes in case the pavement is slippery

What to do

1 Identify all the risks that Justin was trying to avoid.

2 Make a list of any other risks he might face.

3 Draw the items which would help Justin to avoid these other risks.

Everyday Risks

Many ordinary, everyday activities involve risks. For example, when you are standing in the bus queue waiting to catch the school bus you might catch a cold from the person standing next to you. Or you might find yourself standing next to your worst enemy, or get your pocket picked. Or . . .

What to do

Copy and complete the table below. Put four more everyday activities in the left-hand column. Say what risks these activities involve and how they might be avoided.

Activity	Risk	Can this risk be avoided? If so, how?
Walking down stairs	Falling down	Tie up shoe laces. Look where you step. Hold the hand rail.

What to do next

A newspaper has offered a prize of £10 000 to anyone who can get through a normal day without taking a single risk.
Describe how you would attempt to win this prize.

Risky Work

What to do

Oral work in pairs or in small groups

1 What risks are involved in the following activities:

Bathing a dog	Sticking down floor tiles
Painting a gutter	Using weed-killer
Changing a plug	Cooking chips
Using a chain saw	Moving a piano
Making toffee	Dancing at the disco

2 What do you think is the most dangerous job in the world?

3 Which dangerous jobs would you *never* do?

4 Which dangerous jobs *would* you do?

5 What sort of wages would you expect for these jobs?

6 You work for the Risky Jobs Employment Agency. Your job is to find people who are willing to do very dangerous jobs.
Prepare a set of about 10 questions that you would ask someone who came to your agency looking for work.
Then role play an interview at the Risky Jobs Employment Agency using this set of questions.

Changing Risks

As we get older the risks we are exposed to change. For example, we all get ill at some time in our lives. But the risk of becoming ill changes as we age.

Here is an illness 'risk curve'. It shows how the risk of illness changes across our life-span.

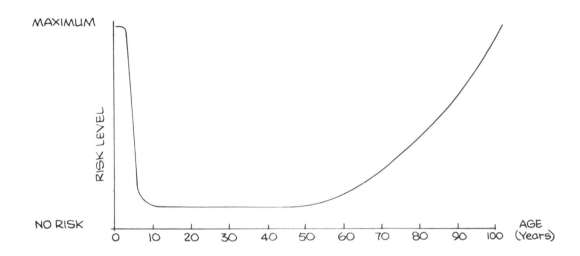

Babies have to build up defences against infection. So for a few years there is a high risk of illness. This risk drops as we get older. It will rise again (slowly) as we reach middle age – about 40 years old. Then it will rise again more steeply as we move into old age – 80 to 90 years old.

What to do

Draw a risk curve:
1   To show the risk of being knocked down in the street.

2   To show the risk (for both sexes) of becoming pregnant.

3   To show the risk of being struck by lightning.

4   To show the risk of getting lost in your home town.

5   To show the risk of getting mugged.

What to do next

Think of two more situations and draw risks curves for these.

13

Risky Sports

What to do

Copy and complete the table below. Add as many other dangerous sports as you can to your table and indicate the risks involved in doing these.

Sport	Risks involved			
	broken bones	**head injury**	**drowning**	**others**
1 Rock climbing	✓	✓		exposure
2 Motor bike racing	✓	✓		burns
3 Wind surfing				
4				

Who picks up the pieces?

Lots of sports are very dangerous. If you take part in a dangerous sport you put your own life at risk *and* the lives of others. For example, if you go pot-holing and get trapped in a cave, someone has to risk their life to get you out. And what about the doctors and nurses who have to pick up the pieces after a motor racing crash? How do you think they feel? People who do these dangerous sports are thoughtless and selfish. These sports should be banned.

What to do next

Working in small groups

1 Do you agree or disagree with the statement above? Give your reasons for this.

2 Think of as many reasons for and against the banning of such sports as possible.
   (These ideas can be used to start a class debate on this issue.)

15

A Different Kind of Risk

A

It's no use being frightened of life. You've got to get stuck in, have a go! You might fall flat on your face, but most people don't. You've got to take a few risks or you end up doing nothing, going nowhere, stuck in a rut.

You take a huge risk getting married. You've got no idea if it will work out or not. And you take an even bigger risk having kids!

B

C

You don't have to take risks. I never do. You can plan your life, just like you plan a holiday, or a party. You don't have to stick your neck out. You can run your life as you'd run a business. Only an idiot takes risks.

When I was sixteen I left school without any exams. My mum said I was stupid to take such a risk. But now I own my own shop. You'll never get rich unless you are prepared to take risks.

D

E

Every time you get to know someone new you take a risk. That person could love you or hate you. But you'll never know unless you risk saying 'hello'. Every new friendship has its risks.

What to do

1 Say if you agree or disagree with each of the five statements opposite. Give your reasons for this.

2 Describe a time when you (or someone close to you) had to take a risk in a relationship with family or friends.

What to do next

To all 4th and 5th year pupils
Can you help?
Some 1st and 2nd year pupils are having problems at school and at home. They need someone to chat to during breaks and lunchtime. I asked them if talking to one of the teachers might help, but they told me that they would rather talk to older pupils.
Will you help?
If you would like to be a 'Helping Hand' please see me as soon as possible.
Ms Byrom
Head of Lower School

Answer these questions. Give reasons for your answers.

1 Do you think first-year and second-year pupils in your school need a scheme like this?

2 If your school had such a scheme would you like to be a 'Helping Hand'?

3 Should anyone who wants to be a 'Helping Hand' be allowed to join the scheme or should there be some kind of 'test' to see if they are suitable?

4 What sorts of problems do you think the first-year and second-year pupils would want to discuss?

5 Why do you think the first-year and second-year pupils asked for help from other pupils rather than their teachers?

No Laughing Matter

1 **Husband:** I've got two tickets for the theatre, dear.
Wife: Oh good. I'll get ready at once.
Husband: Yes, do. The tickets are for tomorrow night.

2 **Mother:** Go and wash your face.
Son: Why?
Mother: Granny won't want to kiss you if you have a dirty face.
Son: That's what I was counting on.

3 **Harry:** Does your wife drive your car?
Larry: No, it looked like this when I bought it.

4 **Mother:** Fred, why did you put this frog in your little sister's bed?
Fred: Because I couldn't find a mouse.

5 **Q:** Why do we call English our 'mother tongue'?
A: Because fathers so seldom get to use it.

6 **Q:** What are the three quickest ways to spread news?
A: Telephone, telegraph and tell a girl.

7 Policeman: Lady, do you know you were doing 75 miles an hour back there?
Lady driver: Isn't that wonderful. I only passed my test yesterday.

8 Q: What's the difference between a girl and an umbrella?
   A: You can shut up an umbrella.

9 (Two boys met in the street. One was leading a bulldog on a lead.)
First boy: 'Look what I got for my girl-friend.'
Second boy: 'Who was stupid enough to do a swop like that?'

10 Mechanic: I've fixed your car.
Woman: How much?
Mechanic: Two pounds.
Woman: That's cheap. What was wrong with it?
Mechanic: It needed petrol.

What to do

Oral work in pairs or in small groups

1 All these jokes have one thing in common. What is it?

2 Many people say that jokes like these are just 'harmless fun' and nobody should be upset by them. Why do you think some people disagree with this point of view?

3 Do you think there are some things that we should **never** joke about?

True or False?

1 Boys are stronger than girls.

2 Girls are not as logical as boys.

3 Girls are no use at dangerous sports because they won't take risks.

4 Girls don't get on in most jobs because they are not as practical as boys.

5 Girls are just as competitive as boys.

6 Girls and boys may behave differently but they are just the same deep down.

What to do

Do you agree or disagree with these opinions?
Write your answer like this for each of the six opinions.

1 I agree/disagree with this because .....

Who Says We're Not?

Dave: Why are girls no good at practical things, like engineering?
Keri: Who says we're not?
Dave: Well, you don't see very many women car mechanics, do you?
Keri: There are lots in Russia.
Dave: I'm talking about here, not Russia. Girls are just no good at practical stuff.
Keri: You're talking rubbish, Dave, as usual.
Dave: Well, I can prove I'm right.
Keri: How?
Dave: We'll do an experiment.

Dave's experiment

Dave asked 20 of his classmates to take part in his experiment, 10 girls and 10 boys.

He got them all to build a model crane out of Lego. Each person was given the same number of pieces to build with and they were all given just 15 minutes to make their crane.

All the boys made a good crane that worked. But only half the girls built cranes that worked well.

The next day Dave told Keri the results of his experiment.
Dave: You see, Keri, I told you I could prove that I was right and you were wrong.
Keri: Your experiment doesn't prove anything.
Dave: Why not?
Keri: Because . . .

What to do

1 What do you think Keri said next? Why do you think she said Dave's experiment 'doesn't prove anything'?

2 'Girls are more artistic than boys.' How could you try to find out if this statement is true or false? Design an experiment that you could do with your class or group to investigate this issue further.

Who Tells Who?

When something was bothering my mother she whistled. She couldn't whistle to save her life and she only knew one tune, 'Yellow Submarine'. But when she had something on her mind she whistled. That night, the night before my fifteenth birthday, she was standing at the kitchen sink whistling.

I was sitting at the kitchen table trying to do my Maths homework. The whistling stopped.

'Dry these pans for me,' she said, throwing me a tea towel.

I went and stood next to her. It was dark outside and I could see her face reflected in the window behind the sink.

The whistling started . . . then stopped again.

'Any minute now,' I said to myself. I thought she was going to have a go at me about my school report.

She said, 'Has he told you yet?'

'Who? Has who told me what?'

'Your teacher. Your Biology teacher. Mr What's-his-name?'

'Mr Simpson?'

'Has he told you yet?'

Then it hit me, like walking into a lamp-post. She wasn't talking about my report. She was talking about sex.
'Well?' she said, 'has he?'

'Oh . . . yeh . . . yeh,' I said, 'we've done all that. Last year. We're on to . . . er . . . osmosis now.'

'Osmosis?'

'Yeh.'

She passed me a cup (she had washed it at least four times) and started whistling again.

Three cups later the whistling stopped. She said, 'What did he tell you?'
'Everything.'

'Everything? Are you sure?'

I nodded.

'There's nothing you want me to tell you?'

'No, nothing.'

'Or your dad? Would you rather . . .?'

'No, honest. We've done all that.'

'Well you'd better get back to your books then,' she said, taking the tea towel from me, 'I want that homework finished before you go out tonight.'

I sat down at the table again and tried to finish my Maths. For once I couldn't make any sense of the figures. I sat staring at them for a while, then went up to my room.

Downstairs my mother was still whistling . . .

*   *   *

Twenty years on, and now I'm standing at the sink. My daughter is fourteen tomorrow.

What will she say when I ask her that same question? Will she think me stupid, old-fashioned, nosey? Is this the right time? Have I left it too late? At her age I thought I knew everything, but really knew nothing.

Now I know just what my mother went through. And I'm the one whistling 'Yellow Submarine' . . . quietly!

What to do

Oral work in pairs or in small groups

1 Why do you think the parent in the story was nervous about discussing sex with her daughter?

2 What can a young person do to help if their parents are nervous about discussing sex?

3 What point do you think the story is trying to make about parents, children and sex?

4 Only 1 in 10 young people are told about sex by their parents or guardians. Most find out about sex from friends, older sisters and brothers and through sex education lessons at school. What might be the advantages and disadvantages of asking the following people for advice on sex:

Parents   Agony aunts/uncles (in magazines)

Older brothers and sisters   Teachers

Friends

5 Who else might give a young person good advice and accurate information about sex?

Quinton

On a recent expedition into deep space, astronauts from Earth discovered a strange planet called Quinton.

Quinton is about the same size as Earth. It has the same atmosphere, the same plants and animals. The people on Quinton look rather like people on Earth. But they are very different from us in one way. Here on Earth we have just two sexes, female and male. On Quinton they have five sexes.

On Earth we have women and men. But on Quinton there are steks, hofs, dats, glods and zanes.

The astronauts were able to study these five sexes and brought back the following information.

Steks
Steks are tall and strong. They are very active. Many join the army. Most marry young. They are good at sewing and singing. They bear children, but not before they are about 30 years old. Most steks have three children.

Hofs
Hofs are very religious. They are gentle and talkative. They are not very emotional. They think of themselves as superior to the other four sexes on Quinton.

Dats
Dats look after the homes and bring up the babies. They can't have children themselves but work for others who can. They are self-confident and ambitious. They are clever and strong.

Glods
Glods cry very easily. They can have children but rarely do. They are natural leaders. They are good at making decisions. They like painting and poetry. They are neat and tactful.

Zanes
Zanes bear many children, but most zanes are engineers working away from home. They are rather bossy, always ordering the other four sexes about, especially hofs.

What to do

Oral work in pairs or in small groups

1   If you had been born on Quinton which of the five Quinton sexes would you like to be?

2   If we had five sexes here on Earth (instead of just female/male) how do you think this would affect your life?

    What difference would it make to school life?

    What difference would it make to families and marriage?

What to do next

Writing

If a group of athletes from Quinton came to Earth for the Interplanetary Olympics, how do you think they would react to life on Earth?

Imagine you are one of these visiting athletes from Quinton.

Write a letter home describing your first meeting with 'Earthlings.' Your letter should mention the shock you got when you discovered there are only two sexes on Earth.

Janet and John

A psychologist wanted to study the way people react to babies. She wanted to know if the sex of a baby has any effect on the way people react to it. She did a simple experiment to investigate this.

The experiment

She took her own baby girl, Janet, out in a pram. She stopped twenty people in the street and said to each of them, 'This is my baby girl, Janet. What sort of baby do you think she is?' The twenty people described Janet as cute, lovely, attractive, bonny, pretty, sweet, gorgeous, charming and attractive. The next day the psychologist took her baby out again. She stopped another twenty people in the street. But this time she said, 'This is my baby boy, John. What sort of a baby do you think he is?'

The twenty people now used words such as bouncing, cheeky, healthy, strong, playful and mischievous when they described the baby.

Same baby. Two very different sets of words.

What to do

How would you explain the results of the psychologist's experiment?

Here are four possible explanations. Say what you think of each one. Write your answers like this:

Explanation 1   I think this is a good/bad
                 explanation because......

Explanations

1   Baby boys and baby girls do not look the same. So people are bound to use different words to describe them.

2   People like baby girls more than baby boys. So they use nice words like 'bonny' to describe girls and words like 'mischievous' to describe boys.

3   Baby boys are very active. Baby girls just lie in their prams and smile. This is why people use different words for boys and girls.

4   Women are much nicer than men. They don't fight, drink and swear like men do. This is why most people think baby girls are more gentle and more attractive than baby boys.

What to do next

You have been asked to take part in an experiment. You have to observe 20 babies. They are all playing together in a large room full of toys. They are all dressed exactly the same. You do not know their names or anything else about them.

Your task is to observe the babies and decide which are boys and which are girls.

Make a list of the things you would look for in their behaviour or actions to help you make up your mind about the sex of the babies.

Once upon a time

Kito's Stones

Once upon a time there was a boy called Kito. He was a strong brave boy, who feared nothing. He had a sister, Lu-chan, who was pretty and kind.

One day Kito and Lu-chan were looking after their father's goats. The two children sat on the grass by a small lake. 'Let's have lunch,' said Kito.

So Lu-chan opened her basket. Inside was a blackberry pie their mother had made especially for them.

Just then they heard a loud grumbling noise.

'What's that?' cried Lu-chan, her eyes wide with fright.

'Don't be afraid,' said Kito, 'it's only Fire Mountain talking to itself.'

Fire Mountain was an extinct volcano that overlooked their father's farm.

Suddenly the ground started to shake.

'Oh the Giants are coming to eat us!' cried Lu-chan.

The Goat Stones

Once upon a time there was a girl called Lu-chan. She was a strong brave girl, who feared nothing. She had a brother Kito, who was also brave and kind.

One day Kito and Lu-chan were looking after their parent's goats. The two children sat on the grass by a small lake. 'Let's have lunch,' said Kito.

So Lu-chan opened their basket. Inside was a blackberry pie their father had made especially for them.

Just then they heard a loud grumbling noise.

'What's that?' cried Kito, his eyes wide with fright.

'It's only Fire Mountain talking to itself,' said Lu-chan.

Fire Mountain was an extinct volcano that overlooked their farm.

Suddenly the ground started to shake.

'Oh the Giants are coming to eat us!' cried Kito.

'Don't be silly,' said Lu-chan, 'there's nothing to worry about.'

Lu-chan was worried, but she did not want to alarm her brother.

'Quickly,' she said, 'we must take the goats home to the barn.'

The two children drove the goats back towards the farm. But before they could reach home their way was blocked by a river of boiling mud that bubbled and hissed like a cauldron.

'Don't be silly,' said Kito, 'there's nothing to worry about.'

Kito was worried, but he did not want to alarm his sister.

'Quickly,' he said, 'we must take the goats home to the barn.'

The two children drove the goats back towards the farm. But before they could reach home their way was blocked by a river of boiling mud that bubbled and hissed like a witch's cauldron.

'Oh Kito,' sobbed Lu-chan, 'what are we to do? We will never reach home! If we try to cross this river of mud we will burn up like paper.' But Kito had an idea. He drove the goats into the mud. They struggled and kicked but soon got trapped in the mud.

'Quickly,' cried Kito, 'jump up on my back!'

Lu-chan did as he said. Then he used the goats as stepping stones and crossed the stream of boiling mud with Lu-chan on his back. Then he carried her home, singing all the way.

Now if you go to the valley where Kito lived you will see some stepping stones across the stream there. Local people call them Kito's Stones.

'Oh Lu-chan,' sobbed Kito, 'what are we to do? We will never reach home! If we try to cross this river of mud we will burn up like paper.' But Lu-chan had an idea. She drove the goats into the mud. They struggled and kicked but soon got trapped in the mud.

'Quickly,' cried Lu-chan, 'jump up on my back!' Kito did as she said. Then she used the goats as stepping stones and crossed the stream of boiling mud with Kito on her back. Then she carried him home, singing all the way.

Now if you go to the valley where Lu-chan and Kito lived you will see some stepping stones across a stream there. Local people call them The Goat Stones.

What to do

Kito's Stones and *The Goat Stones* are two versions of the same folk tale.

Certain changes have been made to the story in the more modern version: *The Goat Stones*. Make a list of these changes. Say why you think the writer of the modern version made them.

29

The Invasion

On 29 July 2042 the planet Earth was invaded by a powerful alien force. First they landed in New York and took over the United Nations building. Then alien craft landed in all the other major cities of the world.

The aliens told the world's leaders that unless people on Earth obeyed their orders they would be killed. This message was broadcast world-wide by radio and television.

Meanwhile, the cruise ship *Fortuna* was in the middle of the Pacific Ocean. When the captain told them the news some passengers voted not to return home. They asked him to take them to a deserted island and he agreed.

On 31 July 1992 the *Fortuna* dropped anchor off an uninhabited Pacific island. Ninety-six people went ashore. The captain gave them some food and water, then the *Fortuna* sailed away.

The people made big fires from driftwood and spent their first night on the island sleeping on the beach.

In the morning the people talked about what they should do next. They began to argue. Nobody could agree on what to do, then someone said, 'Let's make a list and vote on it.'

This is the list they made:

A Make huts from grass and trees.

B Dig some holes in the ground to catch rain water.

C Share out the food.

D Explore the island.

E Search for some more food.

F Make some weapons.

G Elect a leader.

H Catch some fish.

I Look for water.

J Pray for strength and guidance.

What to do

Rank the 10 actions above from 1 (to be done first) to 10 (to be done last).

Compare your list with that of others in your group.

Make a list of the actions that came high in other people's lists.

Add anything else you think the people on the island should have done.

What to do next

Each person brought two or three suitcases from the ship. These cases were full of clothes and other personal items.

It was cold at night on the island. Some people had a lot of warm clothes. Others had none. Someone said, 'Why don't we pool all the clothes, then share them out fairly?'

This started another argument. Three different ideas were put forward:

A Put all the warm clothes in one big pile. If people are cold during the night they can go and get some extra clothing.

B Give all the warm clothing to the older people who need it most.

C Only give warm clothes to sick people.

What do you think of these three suggestions?

Write your answers like this:

1 I think suggestion A is good/bad because.....

31

One or Many?

Two days later the group was still on the beach. One of the group, a 67 year-old man, had died. One small child was ill. Half the water they had been given by the captain of the *Fortuna* had been used.

People argued and argued about what to do. A meeting was called and everyone gathered round one huge fire.

A woman stood up and said, 'I think we should split up into smaller groups. We don't get anything done as we are. The group is too big. Nobody listens. People just argue all the time. It's like trying to run a football team with 90 players and no captain.

'Nothing gets done. Nobody does anything. We should organise ourselves into groups of 5 or 6. Each group could look after itself. If a group works hard, looking for food, making a shelter, then it will survive. If another group is lazy and sit in the sun all day, doing nothing, then they won't survive. We could be on this island for years. We've got to organise ourselves or we won't survive. And the best way to organise is to split up into small groups.'

Then a man stood up and said, 'I think she's wrong. What she is saying is just like the law of the jungle: that only the strong will survive. What about the old and very young, and the people here who can't cope? We can't just forget about them. We must stick together. We will be stronger if we stick together. There may be animals we could trap for food on this island. We've got more chance of doing that if we hunt as a team. We might never catch anything if we go hunting in twos or threes. So only the strongest hunters might get enough food. No. We must stick together and work as one unit. We must never split up. Never!'

What to do

Oral work in pairs or in small groups

1   Which of these statements is the best summary of the woman's argument?

   A   Large groups talk too much.

   B   Large groups will not survive.

   C   Large groups are more difficult to organise than small groups.

   D   Small groups are stronger than larger groups.

2   Which of these statements is the best summary of the man's argument?

   A   A large group will be better at hunting than a small group.

   B   One large group will work as a team and take care of everyone in it.

   C   The law of the jungle means large groups are stronger.

   D   The people on the island must never split up.

3   Who do you think put forward the best argument, the woman or the man?

4   If you had been on the island and had joined in the argument, who would you have supported and what would you have said?

What to do next

Writing

1   Make a list of the qualities a person would need to survive on the island. Write your list in a table like the one below, and give reasons for the qualities you have chosen.

Quality	Reason
Courage	They may have to face many difficult and dangerous situations

2   List the qualities that make someone a good leader. Think of a person you know, someone in your family or a friend, who would be a good leader. Use your list to write 5 or 6 sentences describing how this person might cope with life on the island.

Water

One week later there were only 200 litres of fresh water left. Three groups had gone off into the jungle to look for water but they had found none.

A meeting was called to decide what to do. Everyone agreed that the water must be strictly rationed. The following ideas were put forward:

A   Everyone should have only half a cup of water a day. But very young people and sick people should have a double ration.

B   Everyone should have the same daily ration.

C   Nobody should be allowed to drink during the day when it is very hot. Water should only be given out at night, so people will drink less.

D   How much you get should depend on your age. The older you are the bigger your ration.

E   How much you get should depend on your height. The taller you are the bigger your ration.

What to do

Oral work in pairs or in small groups

1   Are any of the five ways of rationing water given above fair?

2   If you had been in charge of rationing, how would you have shared the water?

The Split

Two weeks later there was a very serious argument over the food. Another old person had died and two more children were sick.

Yet another meeting was called to try to solve the group's problems. But this only made matters worse.

Eventually the people on the island split into two groups. One group went off to live at the north end of the beach, about 15 km away. The other group stayed at the south end of the beach.

The two groups were as follows:

At North Beach

Total number of people in the group	70
Number of males	20
Number of females	50
Number of persons age under 5	11
5 to 15	20
16 to 30	4
over 30	35

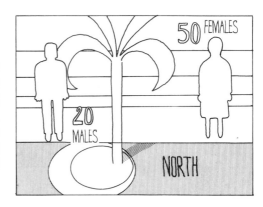

At South Beach

Total number of people in the group	24
Number of females	14
Number of males	10
Number of persons age under 5	0
5 to 15	2
16 to 30	14
over 30	8

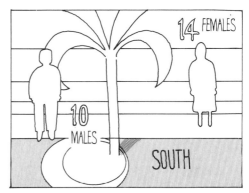

What to do

Oral work in pairs or in small groups

1 Nearly half the North Beach group were under 15 years of age.
  Would this affect the group's chances of surviving?

2 Nearly three-quarters of the North Beach group were women and girls.
  Would this affect the group's chances of surviving?

3 Which group do you think had the best chance of surviving on the island, the North Beachers or the South Beachers?

What skills?
In the South Beach group there were:

2 electrical engineers	1 newsagent
1 painter and decorator	2 bus drivers
1 nurse	1 stunt woman
1 art teacher	1 builder
1 psychiatrist	1 police officer
2 shop assistants	1 musician

What to do

Oral work in pairs or in small groups

1   Which of the South Beach adults had skills that would help their group to survive?

2   If you had been one of the South Beach group, what skills would you have tried to learn? Try to think of a skill that the others in the group did not have.

What to do next

Writing
Choose any two people from the list above, e.g. the nurse and the builder, and write the conversation that they might have if they argued over who had the most useful skills to offer the group.

Twenty years later

During all this time there had been no sign of the aliens. No ships had passed near the island and no planes had been seen overhead.

Both groups on the island had found water. The North people had discovered a spring and the South people had dug a well. Both groups killed and ate animals in the jungle and caught fish in the sea.

The two groups lived completely separate lives. Each group kept to its own half of the island. Each group had its own way of doing things, its own laws and beliefs.

Life in the North

All the leaders in the North were women. Women made all the decisions. Men did all the work, such as fetching water and getting food or firewood.

People in the North could only have children if they were married.

People could only be married if the leader agreed to it. Couples could only have one child.

There were strict laws in the North. Murderers were taken out into the jungle, tied to a post and left for the wild animals. Thieves had heavy logs tied to their feet for five years.

All children were taught to read and write. But only girls got a better education.

Life in the South

The people in the South were led by one particular family. This family had dug the well. They had saved the group by finding water. To be a leader you had to belong to this family.

People in the South had laws too. They could only be married when they were 25 and then only with the blessing of the Well People.

Murderers were sent to live alone in a cave in the centre of the island for the rest of their lives.

Thieves had a device, made of bone, fitted to their chin. This allowed them to eat and drink. But it stopped them talking.

Only those children belonging to the ruling family – the Well People – were educated.

What to do

Oral work in pairs or in small groups
1 If you had been on the island, would you rather have lived in the North or in the South?

2 How do you think the following crimes would have been dealt with in the North and in the South:

Murder   Rape

Theft   Drunkenness

Cruelty to children

Role play
The class should divide into two roughly equal groups. The two groups should improvise a courtroom scene to show how the following problem might be dealt with in the North and in the South:

An unmarried woman has had a child. Two men claim to be the father of this child. One of the men has stolen the baby. The other man has threatened to kill the child and the mother.

A Ghostly Silence

One hundred and fifty years later

The aliens had left the Earth. Many of them had been killed by a strange virus. Slowly the peoples of the Earth took control of their lives again. Two centuries of slavery were over. In January 2192 a survey ship from New Zealand came to the island. It was looking for oil.

The crew landed on the same beach where the passengers from the *Fortuna* had come ashore. On a grassy bank near the shore they found a circle of human skulls, 20 metres in diameter. There was nothing else left of the South people's village. Not a pot or pan or plough.

When they walked north they came to the North Beach settlement. They found seven square houses, in a circle round a large flat stone. The village was deserted. Inside the houses the survey crew found clothes, flutes, weapons, jars of water, stores of fresh food, including some fish. All the beds were neatly made. There was ash in all the fireplaces, but it was cold. A ghostly silence hung over the village.

What to do

Oral work in pairs or in small groups
The crew of the survey ship had no idea what had happened to the people from North Beach. They thought any one of the following might have happened:

A   All the people in the village had been killed by wild animals.

B   They had all died of a mysterious disease and were buried in the circle of skulls.

C   They had all run away when they saw the survey ship coming and were hiding in the jungle.

D   The aliens had taken them away as slaves when they left Earth.

E   They had all left the island on rafts to try to find other people on other islands.

1   Discuss the five explanations above and decide which one seems the most likely.

2   What other explanations are possible?

3   What sort of evidence would the crew of the survey ship have needed to be able to say for *certain* what happened on the island?

What to do next

Writing
You are a member of the crew on the New Zealand survey ship. You spent a week exploring the island. During that week you kept a diary. You made sketches of things you saw and notes about your thoughts and feelings, as you walked about the empty island.

Write your diary. Include some drawings of any interesting things you saw and a sketch map showing the places you explored.

The circle

The survey crew stayed on the island for a month. One of the crew took a closer look at the circle of skulls at South Beach. She found a small wooden box buried in the centre of the circle. In the box was an old shirt, a small gold ring and the plastic handle from a suitcase.

There was a message written on the shirt. The cloth was rotten and the ink had faded. The message read:

> South Beach July 2183 or 4. Today we buried the last of them. They are all here now. We were not to blame. You must know that, we were not to blame. We did not start the killing. We could have lived in peace. They crossed the line. The water was for everyone. All our children, not just theirs.
>
> If you find this you will know what we did and why.

What to do

Answer the questions below. Give reasons for your answers.

1   Who do you think wrote the message?

2   Who do you think was buried in the circle of skulls?

3   What do you think happened to these people?

4   Why do you think the ring and the suitcase handle were put in the box with the message?

staff only
TORQUAY
Waiting Room
Ladies
SAVE A DAY
WILLES
BABY CARRY ALL
FEEDING BAG
FIZZ
You'll NEVER walk ALONE

What's Going On?

You are in a railway station waiting for a train. You see these 10 things happening:

1. A woman walking up and down the platform.
2. A man tying a small girl's scarf.
3. A guard going into the Staff Office.
4. A girl bursting into tears.
5. Two people unpacking their rucksacks.
6. A porter running after three children.
7. A policewoman standing in a doorway.
8. Two people singing 'You'll never walk alone'.
9. A woman photographing the rails.
10. A teenager sticking a postage stamp onto the platform.

What to do

People's motives (the reasons why they do things) are not always easy to work out.

Oral work in pairs or in small groups

1. Try to think of a motive for each of the ten actions listed above. (*Why* were these people doing what they were doing?)
   e.g. The woman was walking up and down the platform to keep warm.

2. Pick out five more people from the picture and say *what* you think they are doing and *why*.

What's He Up To?

He's washing his car because it's dirty, isn't he? But he might be doing it because:

A   He wants to be outside to see what is going on in the street.

B   The car is stolen and he is cleaning it before he resprays it.

C   He always cleans the car at 11.15 am on Sunday even if it's perfectly clean.

D   He wants to put off painting the kitchen.

E   He has cleaned it once already, but he has lost his memory.

F   He knows that water will be rationed next week because of a drought.

G   He is doing a sponsored car wash for charity.

Writing

Which of the motives in the list on page 44 is the most likely to cause the man to wash his car?

Which is the most unlikely?

Draw a table like the one below. Rank the motives given in the list from 1 to 7. Put the most likely one first and the most unlikely one last.

Rank	Motive
1	
2	
3	
4	
5	
6	
7	

Compare your table with those of the other people in your group. Try to decide which motive the group as a whole thought most likely.

Oral work in pairs/small groups

1 It is not always obvious why people do certain things. (It is not always easy to understand their motives.) Can you think of any situations when this might lead to serious problems?

2 Do you ever find yourself in a situation where you want to hide your *real* reason for doing something?

3 Can you think of any jobs for which you might need 'motive spotting' skills?

Strangers or Friends?

What's going on?

Here are some suggestions for what might be going on in this picture:

A   These two women may be neighbours who are having a row.

B   They may be strangers. The white woman may be objecting to the black woman sitting on a bench reserved for 'Whites Only'.

C   They may be good friends. The black woman may be imitating her friend's expression as she tells her a story.

D   They may be two film actresses rehearsing on location.

What to do

Is there any evidence in the picture to help you decide which of the four explanations might be true?

Draw a table like this one and complete it.

Explanation	Evidence in picture
A	
B	
C	
D	

You've Got to Suffer . . .

A Why is this person running up and down sand-hills for four hours each day wearing heavy boots?

B Why has this person made a promise never to speak for the rest of his life?

C Why has this person spent six months making a model out of 160 million match sticks?

D Why has this person been lying on a cold, hard London pavement for three days and nights?

What to do

Oral work in pairs or in small groups

1 What do you think motivated the four people above to do what they did?

2 People with very strong motivation will give up a lot to get what they want. What do you think you might have to give up to become:

   A An MP

   B A nun or priest

   C A spy

   D A world champion ice-skater

   E An overseas aid worker with Oxfam

3 What ambitions have you got? What might you have to give up to achieve them?

Mrs Spencer's version of the incident

'I was looking out of my front room window last night about 10 o'clock,
when I saw old Mr Macari crossing the road. A car came into the street
very fast and Mr Macari was nearly run over. He fell down on the street
and I ran out to see if he was all right. I'm a trained nurse and I could see
right away he was just badly shaken. His pulse was normal and he didn't
have any bruises. I helped him into his house. I told him he should go
upstairs to bed. But he wanted to stay in the lounge because it was warmer.
He lay down on the sofa and I covered him with a rug.

'Then I went home to get a bottle of brandy. He wasn't in a state of shock
and I thought a small brandy would cheer him up and make him sleep
better.

'About midnight he asked me if I would stay the night so I went back
home again and got my camp bed and some blankets. Mr Macari couldn't
get to sleep, so we listened to the radio and played cards until quite late. I
think I must have fallen asleep before he did.'

Mr Lawson's version of the incident

Mr Lawson lives across the road from Mrs Spencer.

'She ought to be ashamed of herself. She's a hard-faced bitch, that's what she is. She should have gone for the doctor right away. Old Frank Macari is lucky to be alive. You'd think she would know better, seeing that she used to be a nurse. Or so she says!

'And there she was carrying in bottles of drink. Pretending it was for the patient. But I bet she drank it herself. Any excuse for a booze-up.

'You'd think she would have waited until it was dark before she moved her bed in. The hard-faced bitch. She's after Frank's money you know. He'll never be rid of her now. She'll hang around like a vulture until Frank snuffs it.

'And all that singing and dancing till all hours. Six months I give him. No more. Six months. You mark my words.'

What to do

Mr Lawson thought he knew why Mrs Spencer did what she did. He thought he understood her motives. But he was wrong.
Copy and complete the table below.

What Mrs Spencer did	Why Mrs Spencer did this	What Mr Lawson thought
She didn't get a doctor		
She took drink to Mr Macari's		
She took her bed to Mr Macari's		
She played cards with Mr Macari		
She stayed all night at Mr Macari's		

What to do next

1 Why do you think Mr Lawson thought what he did about Mrs Spencer?

2 Can you think of a time when someone has misunderstood your reasons for doing something?

Getting a Bad Press

Here are six people's opinions of young people today.

1 Mr Holt

> They've got too much money to spend. They never think about people less fortunate than themselves. They just take, take, take. They have it too easy. They get everything handed to them on a plate.

2 Mrs Jenkins

> They're sex mad, all of them. Not just the boys. They're all immoral. They're a bad lot. It would never have been allowed when I was young.

3 Mrs Carter

> I think most teenagers are wicked. But I don't blame *them*. Nobody teaches them right from wrong these days. They don't have religious education like we did. Some of them don't even believe in God!

4 Mr Baker

> They are a disgrace. They never wash. They're all the same – yobs and layabouts. They don't want to work. They don't want to do anything.

5 Mr Parsons

> They're all thugs and hooligans. Decent people can't go out on the streets at night. We were never violent when we were young. Mind you, I blame television for a lot of it.

6 Mrs Woods

> It makes me sick when I read about all these young people going on peace marches and protesting about nuclear weapons. What do they know about peace? They're all communists.

What to do

Oral work in pairs or in small groups

1 Do you think that anything these six people say about young people is true?

2 Why do some people have a low opinion of young people?

3 What can young people do to help other (older) people understand their motives and their problems?

4 What could you say to Mr Holt and the other people pictured opposite to try to change their feelings about young people? Perhaps, for example, you might tell Mr Holt about people from your school who do voluntary work at local hospitals, visit old people at home, etc.

What to do next

Role play and writing

A newspaper reporter is writing a story about a group of residents who are protesting about a local youth club. They say that the club should be closed because club members take drugs, get into fights and vandalize the street.

The reporter wants to give both sides of the story. They arrange three meetings:

A A meeting with some of the residents.

B A meeting with some of the young people from the club.

C A meeting where residents and club members get together.

Role play these three meetings. Make a list of opinions brought out in this role play. Then, using this as a guide, write a newspaper story about the residents' protest and the response to it.

How Old is Old Enough?

Yesterday

Today

At what age should a young person be allowed to do the following:

◀ **Copy this part only** ▶

			Age	Range
1	Go to the corner shop by themselves.	1		
2	Ride a bike on a main road.	2		
3	Buy their own clothes.	3		
4	Drink alcohol at home.	4		
5	Stay up as late as they like.	5		
6	Go on holiday with a girl-/boy-friend.	6		
7	Smoke cigarettes if they want to.	7		
8	Go to a late-night disco with friends.	8		
9	Dye their hair green.	9		
10	Take up rock-climbing or another dangerous sport.	10		
11	Baby-sit for a 3-year-old nephew or niece.	11		
12	Use an electric drill unsupervised.	12		
13	Be left alone in the house all day.	13		
14	Be left alone in the house all weekend.	14		
15	Go on holiday with friends, rather than with the rest of the family.	15		

What to do

Writing

1   Working in pairs, copy the chart opposite. Fill in the left-hand column only, after you have discussed at what ages people should be allowed to do these things.

2   When all pairs in the class or group have filled in the left-hand column, find the range of ages for each of the situations.

Which situation had the biggest range? Can you think of a reason for this?

A happy medium

What to do

Oral work in pairs or in small groups

1   Parents and guardians have to let go sometime. What kinds of problems might arise if parents 'let go' too soon?

2   What kinds of problems might arise if they 'let go' too late?

3   Do you think your own parents or guardians give you enough freedom?

Special? How Special?

> What's so special about being a teenager? Nothing! Always moaning. Always feeling sorry for themselves. They think they are the only people on this planet with problems.

Mrs G Rumble

What to do

Oral work in pairs or in small groups

1   Do you think any of the following present special problems for teenagers:

Money	Making friends
Exams	Self-confidence
Finding a job	Loneliness
Learning about emotions	Fashion
Meeting the opposite sex	Coping with illness and death
Rapid physical changes	Learning to take responsibility

2   Why do you think Mrs G Rumble thinks teenagers are 'always feeling sorry for themselves'?

3   If you met her what would you say to persuade her to change her mind?

What to do next

Writing
Write a reply to Mrs G Rumble's statement. Use some of your ideas from question 1 above, to support your argument.

I Couldn't Do That ... Yes, You Could

What to do

Copy the table and fill it in. Use a number from 0 to 10 to show how confident you would be in the ten situations listed below.

 (0) = not at all confident   (5) = quite confident   (10) = very confident

← **Copy this part only** →

Situations		Rating (0–10)
1 Giving someone instructions on how to find the nearest police station.	1	
2 Bathing a baby.	2	
3 Changing an electrical plug.	3	
4 Making a telephone call to France.	4	
5 Asking a girl/boy you like to a party.	5	
6 Making a meal for your parents or grandparents.	6	
7 Going to the headteacher to ask about a problem at school.	7	
8 Giving a talk to your class/set.	8	
9 Arguing with your parents about politics.	9	
10 Taking a faulty record/tape back to the shop to complain.	10	

What to do next

What situations do others in your class find difficult to cope with?

Do these situations have anything in common?

What makes someone confident?

I think the most important things are good looks and good clothes. If you have those you'll be 100 per cent confident, anywhere, any time.

1

2 Confident people are all people who know where they are going in life. They have a clear plan and they don't let anyone or anything stand in their way.

Money! That's what makes someone confident. If you don't have money, you're a nobody.

3

4 People with lots of confidence all have one thing in common – parents who loved and respected them. You can't feel confident if you don't feel loved.

Confidence is like anything else. You can learn it, like any other skill. It's just like riding a bike or swimming. Anyone can be confident if they have the right teacher.

5

What to do

Oral work in pairs or in small groups

1 Do you agree or disagree with the five opinions given opposite?

2 What do you think gives a person self-confidence?

3 In what sort of situations do you feel confident?

4 In what sort of situations do you lack confidence?

5 What sort of experiences might help a young person to develop their self-confidence?

What to do next

Working in small groups

One half of the class or set should tackle question 1 and the other half should tackle question 2 below. Each group should then compare the two sets of rules and see what common features they have.

1 Write down some rules that **parents** should follow if they want their children to be confident.

2 Write down some rules that **teachers** should follow if they want their pupils to be confident.

Cutting the Cords

At 16 you can leave school, get a full-time job and get married (with your parent or guardian's permission). But leaving home is not so simple.

If you are under 16: you can leave home if your parents agree and you go to live with an adult relative. You can also go and live with an adult, who is not a relative, if your parents and the Social Services department agree. If you leave home and do not follow these rules you are likely to be taken into care.

If you are over 16 and under 17: you can leave home even if your parents don't want you to. If the Police or Social Services department think you are in physical or moral danger, they can take action. They have the power to return you to your home or place you in a Social Services home. Your parents may want you back but the Police and Social Services may not support their demands.

If you are over 17 and under 18: the Police and Social Services have no power to act, even if they think you might be in some danger.

Any young person under 18: is still in the 'custody, care and control' of their parents or guardians. So if parents are desperate to keep a young person at home they can apply to the High Court and try to have them made a ward of court. This is very unusual because it is a complicated and expensive process.

My son Ron is 16 next month. He wants to leave home and go and live in a flat with a gang of punks. Over my dead body!

1 Ron's mum

58

Alison is 15 and wants to leave home. She lives with her dad and has been very unhappy at home since her mum left. She wants to go to live with her Auntie Kath in Blackpool. Kath isn't her real aunt, but they have always been very close.

2 Alison's friend

3 Sharon's dad

Sharon is too young to go off to London on her own. She's not 18 until next month. I told her I would get the police to bring her home if she went. She just laughed. She doesn't seem to care.

Our son moved out last year when he'd just turned 16. We've been trying to get him to come back home ever since. Now he's living with a couple who both have prison records. We're worried sick about him.

3 Mr and Mrs Collins

What to do

Writing
Read the information given opposite on leaving home. Use it to decide how the four problems above might be solved.

Write your answers like this:

1 I think Ron's mum should.....

What to do next

Oral work in pairs or in small groups
1   What are some of the advantages of living at home?

2   What are some of the disadvantages?

3   What sorts of problem might make a young person want to leave home?

Role play
Role play a conversation between a young person who wants to leave home and their parents who want them to stay.

——— I Remember, I Remember ... ———

Four people recall what it was like to be sixteen.

1   Sixteen-year-olds were still children in the early ...'s. I can remember getting my first pair of 'high heels'. My mum made me wear socks with them. Stockings were too grown up and too expensive. I wore the clothes my mother bought for me. I thought of myself as a schoolgirl, not like teenagers today. Make-up was pale pink lipstick and a dab of powder on the nose. Hair-styles came from the local chemist in the 'Home Perm' box. There weren't many television sets in .... Our friends had one so we were able to watch the Coronation live. Because I was only sixteen I was counted as one of the children and had to sit on the floor!

2   When I was sixteen, in ..., I was allowed to go to the Saturday night dance at the Pavilion Dance Hall on the prom. It took me hours to get ready. I put rollers, grips and setting lotion in my hair. Then I dipped my petticoats in sugar and water to make them stand out. Some of my friends wore as many as six sugar-starched skirts!
If it was a high tide and windy then sea spray would wash over the entrance to the dance hall. Then all my hours of careful preparation were wasted, gone before I even set foot on the polished dance floor.

3   I was at a girl's boarding school in .... We walked everywhere in a crocodile, mainly to church. That year a girl came to our school who was a refugee from the Spanish Civil War. I went to stay at her home in the French Pyrenees, for a month. Her mother believed in peace but not in God. She questioned me endlessly as she cooked. Everyone got kisses night and morning. I read love stories in their garden, under the peach trees. That month changed my life. I returned to my school but never again conformed.

60

4 In . . . the bicycle was the King of the Road. But it was not loved by all. My dad said I was lazy when I went down to the village on my bike, instead of walking. My mum said that people who went speeding along our country lanes were a menace. Cycling without lights or with a friend on the cross-bar were real crimes that the village policeman could not overlook. With your bike you could travel all over England. And your Youth Hostel card was your passport to the rest of the world and to freedom.

What to do

Oral work in pairs or in small groups
1   Look at each of the memories in turn and try to find as many clues as you can about the writer and their teenage years.
    Can you work out the sex of the writer?
    In what year (approximately) do you think they were sixteen?
    Did they have a happy adolescence?

2   If you were talking about your memories of life at 13, what sorts of people, events and feelings would you choose to describe that time in your life?

What to do next

Writing
Interview a relative or close friend. Ask them how they remember their sixteenth year.
Write down what they say. Read it to your class or set and see what clues they can pick up about the person you interviewed and their adolescent years.